IN A
Better
PLACE NOW

Karl T. Woods

AuthorHouse™
1663 Liberty Drive
Bloomington, IN 47403
www.authorhouse.com
Phone: 1 (800) 839-8640

Published by AuthorHouse 09/16/2015

ISBN: 978-1-5049-4759-6 (sc)
ISBN: 978-1-5049-4782-4 (e)

Library of Congress Control Number: 2015914533

Print information available on the last page.

Any people depicted in stock imagery provided by Thinkstock are models,
and such images are being used for illustrative purposes only.
Certain stock imagery © Thinkstock.

This book is printed on acid-free paper.

Because of the dynamic nature of the Internet, any web addresses or links contained in this book may have changed
since publication and may no longer be valid. The views expressed in this work are solely those of the author and do not
necessarily reflect the views of the publisher, and the publisher hereby disclaims any responsibility for them.

Contents

Dedicated to my daughter Angela
and my four grandchildren
Imani, Kemar, Ameena and Isaiah
Thank you for bringing me so much joy
I love you all

PREFACE

I should start by saying that this book is not for everyone. It will only reach a small group of people. You may be asking yourself, It's a book of poetry what do I mean? Poetry is light and playful, full of fun and joy, what's not to like. Well, sometimes it is and other times it can be rough and tumble or somewhere in between.

But you picked this book up because you like poetry and want to experience some interesting and different stuff. To you I say thank you, and enjoy.

For those of you who have read my first book *Secrets Of My Heart*, you understand the above statement. Most of the poems in *Secrets Of My Heart* expressed the darker side of life, love and relationships. But as the title of this book suggests, *I Am In A Better Place Now,* and the poems reflect that. They express much more of the joy and happiness as it relates to life, love and relationships. Of course there are a few poem on the darker side because let's face it, relationships are not always rosy.

In writing this book I realized sometimes a person just has to do it their way no matter what the "norm" says or thinks. You know what I mean, take a risk, go out on a limb, think outside the box, go for it, and all that jazz.

It's your thing, your groove, your passions, your heart and desires that are at stake not someone else, yours, so by all means do it your way. And I know if I don't, it will keep me up at night.

There will always be those that cast judgement and doubt. Those who think they can do it better than you. To you I say, stop it, get on with your own project (other the judgement and doubt, of course) do it your way, and remember, there is even someone out there better than you…hum!

The truth is no matter how we slice it, poetry is a medium for a writer to express his or her thoughts. It's a comfortable place for them to rest their head and heart so they can express what's on their mind playful or not. Somewhat like an old pair of jeans we love to slip on and would never dream of getting rid of. A wonderful place they retreat to find solitude, alone with their thoughts and feelings.

The meaning of poetry is different for everyone. Poetry is versus of the heart, mind, spirit and emotions. Poetry is found everywhere and in virtually everything we see, hear, feel and touch. We aren't always aware of it, or look at it from that angle. As human beings we are all poets, believe it or not. You have heard the saying, "you're a poet and don't know it" well, it's true, we all have feelings we can write about don't we? The fact is this is really a form of poetry that we don't express often or want anyone to know about. But that's poetry and truth in motion baby! And if it's in you, just let it come on out.

We all have feelings wrapped around inner secrets we don't want people to know.

But this is what poetry is really about. We just build walls around our heart and feelings for our own reasons. Life can make us play cruel tricks on ourselves from time to time.

While we are busy compromising our relationships because of emotion, we lose the poetic meaning of love. While we are busy compromising our lifestyle because of money, we lose the poetic meaning of life. While we are busy compromising our habits because of our unwillingness to change, we lose the poetry in reality. In essence we lose it all. We become blinded and no longer see the poetic simplicity of life itself.

I enjoy my journey and embrace it at face value with an open mind. I wouldn't have it any other way. And I will keep on writing about my journey because I feel so blessed to be alive. After all, without the challenges I encountered, faced up to and conquered, I would have never grown (grown up).

Thank you for buying my book, and I hope you enjoy reading the poetry of one humble man.

Dad 11/23/96 By Angela Woods

I call you when I need you
And you'll always be there
You saw me come into the world
And you will be with me
As my life goes on
You tell me your problems
And I tell you mine
You're my Dad
And you're one of a kind
When ever I'm around you
I always feel safe
You're the best
And no one can take your place

SPRING FLOWER

Mother

I love you
It's because of you
I am, who I am
We are so much alike
I never told you enough
I love you
But I do and always will
I know, I know I always talk with dad
It's a man thing
You are the one who made us who we are
It's the mother, the driving force
That keeps us whole

Dad

Where can I begin
To speak of a man
Who means so much to me?
Who has done so much for me
Without fail or thought of himself
So many memories give way
Through my sadness of your passing
Dad, it all started from birth
And just got better from there

Dear Sister

This is the hardest time of your life
Dear sister how do I understand
The sorrow and mourning of another
Sometime's, just a heartfelt embrace
Of a loved one is enough
To know we are one in sorrow
Sometime's, it's a kind word
That brings tears of joy and fill your heart
With their love for you
Those who care will find a way
My heart will always
Be in your hands to comfort you
In your time of need whenever the storm
Is more than you can bear alone
Remember this
As you cast your eyes on tomorrow
In Prayer of a brighter day

Gwen

The loss of a matriarch
So pure with such a loving heart
A loss my mind cannot conceive
So young and full of life
Spirit beyond compare
You mean so much to so many
There is no earthly gift
I could give to match
The beauty in your soul
A second Mother with a giving heart
An ear that did not judge
Strong words of encouragement
Tender words of advice
The glue that bonds us all together
I'm thinking of all the fun times
I had growing up with you around
And the cheeseburger's, look out Heaven
Your rapture has come
For those of us left behind to mourn
We know you now walk on streets of gold
In the Kingdom of God

Branch Of Life

Auntie you have passed on
But you leave behind a Spirit
That will live forever in my heart
Growing up you were a second Mother
Your laughter and love
I have always remembered
And will always treasure
I was a spunky kid
Full of pranks and couldn't sit still
But your patience was enduring
Understanding a blessed virtue
Some things a kid never forgets as he get older
The last time I saw you
When I say goodbye, see you later
You looked at me
With your gorgeous blue eyes
And without saying a word
Said I don't think so, I'll be home then
It made me think of Mom and Dad
Who had gone home before you
They were speaking to me as you were
Without saying a word
And somehow at that moment
The look in your eye's
Gave me strength and humility
I don't think you would want it any other way

Guiding Light

I feel I have known you for a lifetime
In the short time I have known you
To see your smiling face each day is a joy
I will always treasure our friendship
Our friendship has grown fast
And what a blessing it has been
When you speak, I listen
I feel your pleasure and pain
I am proud to be a friend you trust and confide in
Your face shows the challenges
That attempt to overwhelm you day after day
But the determination in your heart
The strength of your character
Pulls you through with Grace
Your love for life and family
The compassion in your soul
Help you to rise above and tear down
The strongholds of defeat
Your wisdom touches everyone around you
You are an inspiration
To those who recognize truth and love
May the Grace of God and the Love of Christ Jesus
Continue to Strengthen You, Day by Day

My God

What a gift
From our Heavenly Father
To be woven into meaning and purpose
The talent He gives us
When we are one and the same
Like a Spirit filled preacher
A musician one with his axe
There is but one way
To circumvent the weaker power of man
Christ Jesus!
Pass along the inspiration
Use the talent given to you by God himself

SUNRISE

Speak To Me

If a mountain
Could move and come to me
What would it say?
Yet I go the the mountains
And speak volumes
As if they could speak back to me
What is it about those majestic giants
That draw us in?

White Sand

I searched far and wide to find you
The missing link to my soul
I found you in the right place
It seems at the wrong time
Dreams of what could have been
Have captivated my thoughts ever since
Oh, if time could reverse itself
What pleasure we would share together
What treasures we could behold
The promises we would keep
The adventures that await us
My imagination runs wild
At all the possibilities of us
At the joy we would find in each other
At the excitement life would bestow upon us
On a white sand beach
As we watch dolphins play in the surf
And feel liquid silk on our skin
As we float in the warm water
I am drunk and lost in thoughts of you
Thinking of how much you care for me
Wondering if this is a dream
And I will awake to a world without you
Let me sleep, please don't wake me
Let me dream of white sand and dolphins
You and I playing in the surf
On a beach all our own

OUR BEACH

Stolen Moments

We live to see
The pale green and grey
In the eyes of our soul another day
We find refuse in each other's arms
Stolen moments of 360 degree love
While we wait for better times
Knowing they are in reach
But seem very far away
Each of us selfish in love
Gobbling each up with wanton passion
Moment by moment a little taste at a time
Time and time again
Savoring each occasion we are together
We love each other as though
We are on a perpetual honeymoon
Love that know no end every time we touch
I look forward to our stolen moments
Tucked in our hideaway of sensual equanimity

LONE PALM

Soul Mates

Some say that relationships
Are just too hard to maintain
Nevertheless, I beg to differ
When two struggle for common ground
When strangers try to create
Chemistry where there is none
As if it were a suspect lab project
When lovers lose their direction
Once out of bed
It's a bitch, and then yes, it is hard
Opposites do not attract for long
There is no substance to take root
And graft them into one being
But soul mates have a ease
That flows from their spirit
In the same direction with synergy
It is a natural progression along the same path
With encouragement and admiration
Every step of the way
Genuinely embracing one another's heart
Enjoying life together timelessly
Without the challenges of most
They can dance the salsa with passion
Their bodies connected
At a glance none can tell
Where one leaves and the other begins
Their love stems from real friendship
That has a seasoned understanding
An intrinsic need and desire to be together
The circle of life now complete
They are a whole of one

See It Thru

Seeing you again
Took my breath away, still
After years gone by
My love for you
Has endured
And hope has survived
My love for you
Has found no end
The candle I lit
In my heart for you
Has always burned
Even in your absence
Three words spoken
From your heart to mine
Gives my dream a new birth
Three words spoken
From your soul to mine
Fans the flames of passion
And within the truth
Sets my heart on fire once again
Three words spoken
That I longed to hear cross your lips
Have been worth waiting for
Because I also love you
And there is nothing
That will ever change that

Undaunted Love

Over the years
I thought I knew what love was
I thought I knew what I wanted form love
Always looking for my soul mate
The hopeless romantic stumbling
Over his own feet blind in love and hope
Then one day I met you and everything changed
You were in my life just a moment
Then another day I looked up and saw my whole life
Leading me back to you after years apart
Our love for each other still alive in our hearts
For well over a decade and counting
I enjoy having you in my life now more than ever
I think of you all the time my darling
And miss our synergy when we are apart
We are so beautiful together
I look forward to spending the rest of my days with you
The adventures, the joy and happiness
The growth, and 360 degree love
How exciting after all the years apart
We have waited and wanted to enjoy life together
Tell me my love...what should I do?
Tell me my love...what should you do?

Still Undaunted

My whole life I have been waiting for you
And somehow I knew that
When I saw you across a crowed room
My plan was to not let you forget me
I subtly wore you down, or so I thought
The thing is you felt the same way for me
All along welcoming my admiration towards you
But would not, and could not let on
Those walls around your heart are tough to climb
Now that we are in each other's arms
I feel strange saying this to you
I don't want my passion to scare you away
This is happening so quickly for us
And I know you have a lot on your plate
Tell me my love what should I do?
We both made a twelve year circle
That led us back to each other
Smarter and wiser I like to think
More in love than ever before
Tell me my love what should you do?

Starlight

Beneath your shiny corona
Lies the mysteries of your heart
Somewhere beyond
Unlock the hidden secrets
You hold so dear
Naked heart, passion endures
My life has been blessed by you
Shine my lovely star

In A Moment

I caught a glimpse of you
From the corner of my eye
You were sitting all alone
You appeared a bit shy
You looked at me and smiled
As if you wanted to say hello
Just as quick you got up to go
I wish I knew what you were thinking
At that moment in time
Your gaze was inviting and it intrigued my mind
I wanted to say hello it felt the right thing to do
I thought maybe we would have a break through
And it would have been a doorway into your world
I missed my chance that day in the moment you gave me
I started to call out to you but that seemed somewhat rude
I missed my chance, not because of you
Oh, If I could just see you again, see your beautiful smile
I wouldn't take so long to say hello, I wouldn't take awhile
I hope you will respond in favor and kind
And we will get to know each other
From that moment in time

If I Told You

There is so much I want to say
But I don't want to give you pause
I mentioned I wanted to write you a poem
But I fight the temptation
You tell in words and looks,why not, go ahead
You feel flattered as much as curious
About how I feel towards you
What could I possibly say?
You truly do not understand
The depth of my admiration for you
From the mouth flows the issues of the heart
Words written seem to have more meaning than words spoken
Though neither are shallow or meaningless
The pen seems to express the depth of one's soul
Do you really want my take, do you?
Then stay seated and hold on my dear friend
We need each other, plain and simple
It seems so natural but strange in a way
We are just trying to figure out to what extend
Our hearts speak to one another soft and subtle
Our eye's and ear's see and hear
What our mouth wishes to speak aloud
And our heart's appear to feel
I may be way off base, but this I know for sure
We are both deep thinkers and introspective people
We need to talk, and often, in a quiet place all our own
To let our heart's and mind's commingle
And twist together in truth and trust
Do you really want my take, do you?
The story continues, but not in a poem
The truth and trust I speak of
Lives in our friendship together
That we dare to explore

To My Surprise

After you read your poem
The look on your face was priceless
Your mouth could not express the words
Your heart seemed to feel
Just looking at you
Melted my heart into a puddle of emotion
I thought best to keep to myself
I adore your shy, and bashful nature
But you could not hide your happiness at that moment
Your face lit up with joy and amazement
That I had never seen before
Your reaction made me feel, well
On top of the world, like a star in heaven
As if I had gained a special place
In your heart forevermore
Seems the poem was good for both of us
I enjoy thinking of you my friend
And I do it probably more than I should
I know that must sound strange
You make it awfully hard for me not to
And I know you don't realize it
You are just being you, wonderful you
And that's what I'm talking about
You see, often that's all it takes
What's not to adore about you?
Whoever said life is complicated
Has got it all wrong…It's just that simple

Third Time Is A Charm

There is something to be said for three's
You know, things seem to happen in three's
Act 3, Scene 3
The Sun, Moon and Stars
The Three Bears
The Father, Son and Holy Spirit
Movie Trilogies
You're once, twice, three times a lady
A third poem just for you
Tucked away in a Valentine's Day card
On my goodness, what could that mean?
Have I completely lost my mind?
Or do I just like you lots?
Wow, three questions...and so it goes
Well, maybe I have lost my mind
Because I'm crazy about you kiddo
Even though this poem is a bit whimsical
It is number three, how about that
Happy Valentine's Day

Thinking Of You

When I think of love
I think of you
When I think of the emptiness
In my heart I think of your love
Which can take its place
If we stretch our arms
Into each other's life
Only you my angel
Can fill this void with your love
And bring life to a withering heart

Zazz Me

The fluent sound of music
The joyous sound of love
The innermost feelings
That bring the Soul
Peace and good nature is touched
Move like the wind, float on a dream
Drift with one that I've seen
I've been lifted away, far away
Bound in the good feeling
Spinning, spinning, spinning

Thoughts Of One Man

There is a moment, a split second in time
When the spark of a persons inner sources
Are reached and sent into motion
Before this time there is confusion and disorder
Now there is peace and tranquility
A feeling of joy, a moment of release
Into a world, a mind not of perplexity
But of harmony to all surroundings
It is harmony to life's forces
Its strength and weaknesses
Harmony to all that is know and unknown
Will be accepted and thought upon

ROLLING HILLS

Getting It All Done

You can't sport another person's success
You can't spend another person's money
You gotta get your own
So stay out of your own way
And get it all done
It's what you have, the hand you were dealt
It's what life allow you to do
It's what life allow you to have
Make the best of it
Make it work, doing your best, working the plan
Being thankful for what you have
It's about you and what you can create
Out of thin air and planning
It gets tough doing the right thing
When you're getting lead in the wrong direction
People and their deceiving
People and their squeezing
The life and love out of you
Their money is not in your pocket
Tell them to check theres one more time
Remember, If your step in light
And your soul is weak
You won't stay on your feet

P.U.S.H.

I keep pushing, praying and hoping
Day by day until something happens
I will not go out like a punk
Whining like some sorry excuse of a man
Giving up, rolling over and playing dead
My hopes, dreams and passions
Are all I crave at this point in my life
I am running out of time
I feel my mortality
I have nothing else to reach for

Real Deal

More often than not
It's the simple and small things
That help us define the big picture
Funny how that works isn't it
The big stuff we may see coming
But that small stuff we say don't sweat
And don't see coming around the corner
Can be a son-of-a-gun you know
Kind of hits our blind spot
Then we think of what we have all been told
You know the stuff, we've all heard it
Be kind to other's, love thy neighbor
Like you would love yourself
Hug a tree, kiss a baby, you've heard it all
Those might work for some folks
That keep their world in a neat little box
That doesn't exist other than in their own head
That's cool though, as long as we remember
Some basic principals of real life
Reality is more like take the bitter with the sweet
Some folks are just plain flakey, superficial and narcissistic
So don't get your feeling's hurt
By expecting too much from them
Or asking too much of them
I know, I know, I must sound a bit cynical
However, don't you know someone
That sounds just like that? Don't you?
So relish the simple things
Don't despise the small things
After all, they are the real deal
They will help us grow
Into that big picture show we all call life
Have fun!

CORN STALK

Compromise *(from Secrets Of My Heart)*

It has been said that first impressions
Are summed up in a matter of seconds
In the seconds when we first met
I could feel the glow of your heart
Your intrinsic beauty
Captured me by surprise
Yet seemingly with those seconds
It all disappeared
For reasons good or bad
Known and unknown
Within the seconds and hours of our lives
We compromise within ourselves
Our relationships
Because of emotion
Our habits
Because of our unwillingness to change
Out lifestyles
Because of money
Our realities with fear
Our today
With the haunts of yesterday
We compromise
Why do we compromise
That which lies deep within our hearts
Listen to the songs of your soul
It sings only the love songs of today
And cries for the needs of tomorrow

Compromise #2 — Give Yourself A Break

There is a standard, a code
We all set in our heart
A rule of thumb, a benchmark we aim for
But how often do we find ourselves
Saying I did it again, not again
When will I ever learn
I compromised my own rules
I didn't keep my eyes on the mark
That I set long ago
How much weight can the human spirit endure?
How long before it hits the wall
And breaks into a million sparkling pieces
How much will I compromise?
We often compromise so much of ourselves
For other people, we forget who we are
We are told by society, friends and family
Think of other's and take your eye's off yourself
Tolerate their drama, issues and foolishness
This is true, and good to a point
Where do we draw the line with compromise?
When do we say no to some
And yes to other's and ourself?
Does this make me a bad person
To think of myself once in a while?
To even pose and ponder this question?
How much can one soul endure
Before it can't get back to the middle?
How much will you compromise?
Find the truth within yourself
A heart speaks louder than words

The Last Compromise #3 — Stand Your Ground

I have always said
People will do whatever they want to do
Whenever they want to do it
For as long as they choose
Until they are sick and tired of it
Then they will stop if need be
And not one day before

There will come a day
When our demons will overrun us
And we will have to stand our ground
Or be consumed by them
How long it takes is up to life, and us

Life events shape and direct our journey
Sooner or later we will reach the point
We have to decide which road to take
The high road or the low road

Run, fight, stand our ground, tear down the walls
Stop the bus, reclaim your life, push and shove
Whatever you want to call it
You will reach the last compromise
And have to make the big decision
To adjust the compass of your life

For some it's easy to stand their ground
Stand in truth and keep it real
Our minds can carry us to depths or heights
That we have never seen before, that are unheard of
That we never though would happen to us

What is happening to me you ask
I have never been like this before
I have always been the strong one
It's a gut wrenching and consuming experience

I am at that that point with you
I have hit the wall and have nothing left to give
I pray to find peace, answers, direction and wisdom
This is the only way I can get back to you

Enough

Sometimes enough, is not enough
And you end up right where you started
At the beginning, yet again
You never think you're moving backwards
Until it's too late, enough you say!
Wondering if you are back at start
Or are your wheels just spinning in a circle
It's impossible to move forward, while going backwards
Some things are just meant to be
Then the wall stops you, and you know

Reach

In life's eye I reach for the stars
It's all I know how to do
One day I will reach my dreams
I will live the life I truly imagine for myself
The desires of my heart
Are real and alive with hope
They are set within reach
And when I reach them
On that joyous day
I will kick up my feet
Raise my arms in the air
And shout, Alleluia
At the top of my voice, I did it!
Doing what I do best
Keeping it real
And reaching for the stars

Little by Little

Little by little
I look at life
In measure
Step by step
A building block
To reach an end
I am a finite creature
Looking to Heaven for answers
Appraisal of path taken
Looking back
To learn for my mistakes
Looking forward
Pushing
Trying hard not to end up
Where I started
Knowing nothing will change
Unless it's from inside me

Eye See You

Deep within the hollow
Of my heart and gut
I feel an emptiness and doubt
Of what I am doing, and what is to be
Everyday I ask myself why and how
Has my life become pressed
With so much unease and challenge
I push on, making adjustments along the way
Looking for answers, hoping that what I see
I will discover to be only a misleading image
Presented to the minds vision
Truth and answers are hidden within the vision
And will soon unfold before me.

God's Canvas

The westerly sky was painted
As only God can paint
Brilliant rich blue piercing my soul
Flowing strands of crimson red
Playful orange with a hint of magenta
What a feast arousing my spirit
Looking east and over the mountains
A dim cloud shrouded moon on the rise
Getting brighter by the minute
At this mystical time when light and dark
Try to occupy the same space in time
Don't leave me sunset with your grace and beauty
With you're telling of what a beautiful day
You have provided my weary soul
The old man in the moon speaks loudly
Giving the sun her final due respect
The old man says it's my turn now
To enchant your weary soul and lift your spirit
As the cycle of life continues

DREAMY SKY

Listen Up

It may not always work out
Like you planned
But God
Planned it with what you need
To use His gifts to you
Be patient
To understand is the key
This is a lesson well learned
Wait on God
Listen for His calling

Better Today

May your day
Be filled with love
And promises never broken
A beautiful day is ahead

Natural Love

My love for you comes naturally
From my heart to yours
I can't pretend of something so real
Loving you comes easy
It seems so natural
To come from my heart to yours

Don't Ask

If I ask for more
It may all disappear
So, I don't ask
I appreciate
What I have been given

STILL GROWING

Light The Way

May a candle of love
Stay lit in our hearts forever
To guide our friendship
To a deeper truth
A heart speaks louder
Than words don't you think

Pinky

Your smile
Brings peace
To my heart and soul
Your touch
Always says you care
Your compassion lifts my Spirit
You are always there for me
When I need you
I always thought I knew love
But you showed me I didn't
And with that
Have brought new meaning to my life

Happy Birthday

The moon in heaven
Smiles as you rise
Watching you bring light
To a new and glorious day
You see, you are sunshine from above
Beautiful, majestic, warm and ageless
Always bringing joy to all you touch

Happy Birthday My Darling

TIMELESS

True Friendship Endures

The closeness of hearts
Is what makes a lifetime friendship
Like ours so wonderful
It is a rare thing to find a person
Who will remain a friend forever
The memories friends make together
Grow stronger with each passing day
They live to remind each other
How good it is to be friends
Thank you for knowing
Just what I need at the right time
Thank you for being my friend

Wake My Love

As dawn breaks
I wait for you to arise
To start my day with your smile
You look beautiful when you are asleep
I know it sounds funny, but it's true
And when you're awake, it just gets better
You treat me like a King
And you my darling, are my Queen
I am so blessed you love me
As much as you do.

Sudden Situation

I search my soul
To find words to write
I dare not speak
Lately my pen is dry
But my soul cries out
As the burdens of life
Gather round me
As an old friend
I quietly rejoice
Listening to the words
Of a familiar song
That use to fill my pen
And inspire me to write
Of the issues of life
Lately, I've been thinking of you
In the notes of the music
In the words your pen has scribed
It seems your wit and charm has no bounds
I see your smile in the words
I hear your laughter as sweet music
I sense your presence all around me
I ache for your touch
This fills my pen again
What a joy!
Dare I write of what I feel
Of my desire, admiration and love for you?
I must of this sudden situation

Sunny Day

You're the only life for me
You always make it plain to see
With your special kind of harmony
That you often bring to me
The sun is out and it's here to stay
You make my troubles drift away
And make me feel I'm a part of you

Sincerity

It has been said that
The eyes are the window to our soul
That does have some truth to it
However, a smile can give our eyes
A run for the roses
Your smile drew me into you
From the moment I first met you
And it still does to this day
Your smile lifts my spirit
Gives me hope in a bright today
You have the most warm and sincere
Smile I have ever laid my eyes upon
And you have unsurpassed beauty
To match your beautiful smile
Whenever you are smiling my way
It seems I feel your love for others
I see beyond your borders
And into your world
I wish I could read your mind
And know if you are drawn to me
As much as I to you
This is a secret that should stay in my heart
Your smile and beauty compel me to hug you
Wanting to feel your beating heart against my chest
To stroke your hair back while looking into your eyes
While telling you sweet things of us

I know this can never happen for many reasons
I keep a watchful eye over my imagination
But you are leaving now and I want you to know
That the thought of never seeing you again
Is more than my heart can bear
And worth the risk of letting you know
Just how much you mean to me
My number one

Hermosa

Age is just a number
As the number increases
The fruits of wisdom should show
But life has an irony
That sometimes can not be explained
I know a man my age
Should not think of a woman half his age
The way I think of you
With the weight upon my life at this moment
I can do no less
Thinking of you brings life
To my tattered heart
Your sweet innocence and childish smile
Will forever be on my mind
They reach the depths of my soul
You seem to be unencumbered
By the weight of this world
Though you must have much on your mind
And difficult challenges to face everyday
You have become a breath of fresh air to me
The song of a robin at dawn
The glow of the sun upon the pacific at sunset
You will be missed my dear friend
I shall think of you often
To help lift my weary spirit
To put a smile on my face
And a poem of love in my heart

True Love

Love
If we mix equal portions of
Understanding
Forgiveness
Communication
Caring
Honestly
Openness
Passion
Thoughtfulness
Trust
Chemistry
We will find a bond with happiness
In a state of being
That we will discover to be
True Love
If we just allow ourself
To embrace these feelings
Time and time again
Unconditionally without reservation
We will find the best reward
Life has to offer
True Love

You And I

I want to to be happy
Not sad
I want to smile
Not cry
I want your love
And your sadness
I want your joy
And catch your tears
But most of all
I want us to be together
In peace

QUEEN PALM

Fear Not

You long for the simple times
When life and love didn't push so hard
I know how you feel and what you fear
What's been said has been said
What's been done has been done
The hurt settles into the bones
How long will the past effect our future?
When will the hurt rise to the top
And be skimmed away as a lesson learned
You're afraid
I ask more of you, than you can give
Your eyes and heart tell the story
I'm afraid
That your clinging to the wrongs of the past
Will stop us from moving forward
As if we need one more excuse
Not to grow together, but apart
How can I put back the pieces
Of a broken Spirit and heart
When we react to our frustrations
I try to stay mindful of your daily challenges
That are overwhelming at times
Life is full of challenges for us to overcome
Through it all, our marriage, must rise to the top like cream
Move forward in the same direction, on the same page
And sing the same sweet song of success

The Very End

Some people will sacrifice
Anything to protect
Their small world
They will stunt their growth
By staying in their comfort zone
Lose track of the nuts and bolts of the real world
Live in denial and hide behind the simple
Rather than embrace the hard facts
Growth requires adversity and may be painful
It is sad what they lose of themselves
And more sad what those around them suffer
The emotional blackmail they endure
Living with no true love, hope or inspiration
No communication, no truth and spirit
Being the villain while trying to lead by example
Growing and changing for the better
For the relationships sake to no avail
What a strange and painful existence
What an existence to live and endure
Uphill everyday, steep and slippery
What they do never gets noticed
Just taken for granted with no question
Fighting back the feeling of bitterness and resentment
Continuing to do the right thing no matter what
Along the way to the last stop
To the very end

Not Again

We save pieces
Remnants of the past
Of how good it once was
For us at a given time
We silently hold onto hope for the future
With a steel grip as we feel ourselves
Drifting far apart
What has become of us
Of the life we once had
And the love we once shared?
Where is the spark
That started our journey together?
Now we struggle to find meaning
Me telling you the truth
And you running from it yet again
Not again I tell myself
What must I do to make ground
To make headway
Against your walls of resistance?
I am just a natural man
I have no super powers
And I cannot venture beyond
Human limitations
You must help me if we are to survive
If we are to grow together
What else can a poor man do
But hold on to pieces

Losing You (from Secrets Of My Heart)

A feeling of despair
A feeling of loneliness
A feeling of loss
And the wondering why
We use to love with passion
Which seems to be all but gone
Now we wonder of love itself
We hold the key in our hearts
The key to lock the door
Of the fear we face
And let it go forever
The key to understand
Why this is happening to us
Some things are up to me
Some up to you
But not knowing why
Is the worst torture of all
Should I continue to love you?
That would be easy for me
Do you still love me?
Or am I just a fading memory
Juggling to find a place
In your heart
If you are hurting
As much as I am
Go into your heart
And bring yourself out to me
As I have for you
And we can make it work
Forever more

STORMY # 1

Losing You #2 — Final Plea

It's down to us baby girl
I can't care anymore than I do
If you would just let me in
You would realize you wonder for nothing
You find your escape in doubt
Doubt that isn't real and shows no trust
Play out the feelings in your heart
Listen to what it says
It's been right so many times
Don't listen to your fears
Fear only plunges you further into doubt
And doubt will destroy your realism of truth
And keep us between this rock and a hard place
Which is where you have us both now
Emotions and feelings
Are issues to take seriously
Not as a joke to be toyed with
But heart to heart
Yours to mine
Love to love

STORMY # 2

Looking Back

You spoke to me like never before
You made me to be a bad man
As you walked out of the door
My heart started bleeding girl
As I watched you walk away
You left me a nightmare
Then you were gone to stay
You came back like a thief in the night
To take what you left behind
Remnants of a life you couldn't make right
Remnants of a life you could never find
It's easier to run and hide, easier to walk away
And deal with reality another day
Why, oh why baby do you face life that way
Why, is it easier to deal with us another day
Why, oh why baby when I loved you so much
And all you did was run from my touch
You were quick to say what's wrong
And never what was right
Just don't get cut on the jagged edges of your life
Let's not throw stones on who is right or who is wrong
We both see us getting worse all along
You never believed me when I spoke from my heart
You twisted my words, and got it wrong from the start
You told me I was crazy when I told you the truth
And I didn't know what I was talking about

You had all the proof
When will my heart stop bleeding girl
When will it stop
When will you leave my world baby
When will you walk
It's like that old time game show
Let's beat the clock
And since you ain't talking no more
The bleeding will never stop

LOOKING AHEAD

Catch

Tears in my eyes
Can I find shelter
In your arms
I'm difficult
But not hard to understand
I'm no nuttier
Than the next
But what do I know
I'm my own worse enemy
It seems I hurt everyone
I try to love

Release

Prayer changes things
Prayer gives me peace
In my soul
So all I seek is love
Can't miss
It's just that easy
There is power in prayer

Oh Lord

Lord you give me so much love
And so many blessings
As much as my heart and mind
Can comprehend and handle
If I don't understand and appreciate
What you give me now
How can I cry out for more?

Standing In Truth

You are
Without doubt or exaggeration
One of the
Kindest, sweetest, endearing and interesting
People I have ever met
I admire and challenge anyone
Especially at your age
To stand in truth as you do
You walk in the light of our Lord
You stay steadfast in your faith
Through thick and thin
Pressing toward the mark of a higher calling
As the world tries to pull you from side to side
You are a blessing to all who know you
Your personality exuded light and love
In the often dark world that surrounds us
You bring laughter, life and joy
To everyone around you
You don't think much of it, it's who you are
And what you unconditionally do
Seeking nothing in return
Except perhaps, seeing a smile on their face
You deserve to be thanked, celebrated and admired
You deserve to be lifted up and encouraged
You deserve to know that someone notices
And is very, very thankful for you
And I just wanted you to know

SUN AND SEA

Thank You

Though there is distance
Between us once again
The measure of love in our hearts
Keeps us close together
You observed the distance
It Is all we have ever known
We agreed the distance
Is what made us strong and trusting
Learning of ourselves
Word by word
Emotion by emotion
And here we are once again
Older, with wisdom on our side
Still able to make each other laugh
Selflessly caring and giving
Our hearts engaged with renewed passion
While longing for a tender embrace
Whatever may come in and of our path
I am thankful for us today
I am thankful for the road we traveled in years past
And appreciate our new road today
The road we travel now
Will lead to an even greater and deeper
Embrace of love and friendship

Weird Love

Some tend to think of love as being perfect
What is perfect in love?
Love is as different
And can be as difficult as life itself
Love can be weird
Love can be strange
Love is always different
And love spares us no exception
Our love was meant to be weird, apparently
Our love was meant to be pure, for sure
Our love was meant to be selfless, what a joy
Our love was meant to be a constant force
In our lives together to strengthen each other
To sing a song of joy
And how wonderfully different our love is
Our love is joyous and rewarding
Nothing weird about that, Amen
If I could change space and time
I would will it so
If I could bridge the mile between us
In a way that would make us both smile
I would will it so
In the meantime, I will embrace our weird love
Because it is ours and I understand it so well
I wrap my arms around our love
Because it is golden and perfect
In a weird sort of way

Last Call

It was inevitable
We both knew the day would arrive
One question was when
Another, who would move first
In making the tough decision
I knew you would fold your hand first
You have always been the stronger of us
Though I was close behind, I think
I lacked the steel to get it done
Perhaps I should thank you
I get it, I understand
It's a though we were being held hostage
By devices of our own making
Our weird love has run deep
And for well over twenty years
But it can only run so long
The emotions at stake are old and frayed
Neither of us want to outlive
The usefulness in each other's life
The hard part for me is feeling
You're still there for me, but not I for you
Maybe I'm wrong, I sure hope so
But during our last talk you all but said it
Our love for each other will endure
However guarded, however silent
It will endure from a distance as it always has
I will always love you, I cannot stop
You have always meant the world to me
And I will always thank God for crossing our paths
For the time and love we shared together
For you just being wonderful you
My God bless you always
My very, very dear friend

Stay Up

The wind carries a voice
Echoes be strong
All is not lost
But the times and situations
Grow beyond enormity
Another day
To live without your love
To realize you have no more to give

Questions Remain

I spoke these words to you
That I see the beauty in your chaos
But it is the weakness in me
That wants to see and understand it
It is my weakness that thinks I can live with it
It is the foolish and blind side of love
The strength in me knows
That I can't live with the chaos
That makes up your life
With you I always give
My time, money and emotion
More than you deserve and appreciate
More than you can handle nor comprehend
It hurts you to give anything
I see it on your face in your vain attempts
And I feel your apprehension
You have not grown up much
And flakey has become your way of life
You view serious matters of life
With no sense of compassion and understanding
And yet, you speak of us with a future
I have come to realize that future
Comes at a heavy price
A price I may not be willing to pay
For so little genuine comfort
Piece of mind and sincerity in return

Final Arrow

I shot my final arrow at you baby
I'm fresh out and they all missed the mark
None made a dent in your heart
I won't let you hold my head hostage
And take up precious real estate
I gotta clear my head of you
As much as you turn me
I can't move or shake you baby
I can't see you and I
And you can't see you and me
I'm just shaking the wrong tree

Stop Lying

Cavort if you must
But that will only play
Havoc in your head
Don't flirt with the truth
As a pawn to be taken lightly
Don't love for the wrong reasons
Admit that to yourself
And by all means possible
Be honest with your lover

Built On Sand

If we can't talk and laugh
About our life and love together
It means we can't grow
We can't move forward
To better place, together
When I truly think about us
And our so-called new and improved
Run for the roses
We are just fooling ourselves once again
How can you say
It's about "our relationship now"
If you are scared to confront the past
If you are insecure to meet head on
What has happened to us before today
It's not dead and buried as you want it to be
It circles around us all the time
Just waiting for the right moment
To rear its ugly head once more
I don't get it, I don't get you
Just something to ponder my dear
Call it soul food for thought

STORMY # 3

Familiar Feeling

When I saw you again
My heart filled with joy
I was nearly speechless
Upon your sudden graceful arrival
Your smile was as warm
And tender as I remember
Your presence was soft and inviting
It bought to mind
Wonderful memories of yesterday
You were even wearing a similar
Flowing summer skirt
As the day we first met
Funny I should remember
It was good to see you
And it would be very nice
To see you again soon

What If

It's a slippery slope we travel
I know you're right, but forgive me
There are no pot holes
In looking at the glass half full
Perhaps I'm wrong, but why not
If I see the glass as being full of you
It will be overflowing with love and joy
Excuse me while I dream of what could be
There is hope in my dream, because of you my darling
There is love in your heart, because there I slumber
If this is wrong, don't wake me, please

In The Night

I wish I could come to you in a dream
Hold you, make love with you
Away from prying eyes and telling lips
I want to feel your desire for me
The desire I see in your gorgeous eyes
When you see the curiosity of passion in mine
Is it my imagination, or is something there
Am I on the right page, in the right book
Or just my wishful meandering mind
I normally see and feel what is real
I have the wisdom of my years
You can't fool me my dear with hidden feelings
Your eyes tell the story of your heart
Though it is possible my vision may be flawed
We both know that us is just wrong
But our glances tell a different story form time to time
Oh the irony of life at work yet again
And so we dance around each other
Staying only so close, guarded, safe and sound
From what we really feel, uttering not a word
Never letting our hearts speak to each other
Just going though the motions as we should
Staying strong, definitely not giving in
To the emotions that bring our hearts together
To the emotions that make our hearts the same

Check Yourself

I'm starting to think
That the woman
I've been writing about
All my years
Comes in a young
Idealistic package
One I should not touch or open
They look at me with eye's they shouldn't
I think of them with thoughts
That can only lead to heartbreak and trouble
If an old man thinks a young woman
Is the answer to his relationship dreams and desires
He needs to think twice
I get the she make me feel young part
But beyond that, really
I mean, really

Artist Games

An artist
Strives to be good
Tap the inner self
The left brain to stay sane
While the right brain drives us mad
And endless struggle of check and balance
Our mind ripped to shreds
Trying to find the words
To express our feelings
It's hard to fight the wars of our head
While enduring the battle of our life

Salt Of The Earth

I am the salt of the earth
I labor my days away
As if I was born in a steel town
I don't ask much, just a break now and then
So I can do it all again

I am the salt of the earth
The working poor, the struggling man
Trying to make ends meet while keeping his pride
Out of the pan and into the fire
Don't get burned while trying to make a play

I am the salt of the earth
Move over let me drive
So I can watch life as we pass by
See what I missed while I was away
I live to tell the tale another day

I am the salt of the earth
Living check to check trying to have some fun
Chasing a dollar making a dime
Trying to enjoy a splendid time

I am the salt of the earth
Robbing Peter to pay Paul
Looking for one last shot to connect the dots
To put it all together and make it work

At the end of the day
I am the salt of the earth

Words Of A Poet

You may be asking yourself
Who is this guy, a shrink or a poet?
Maybe a little of both
After all, when you read poetic verses
Doesn't it sooth your mind
And raise your Spirits?
Or perhaps engage you to ask questions?
Maybe a bit of all three

More to Learn

If I write to purge myself
I must have a lot on my mind
Or doing things all wrong
If I really knew what life is all about
I would have stopped writing a long time ago

KEEP SHINING